AGENCY QUOTES

VOLUME 1

by Nick Entwistle & Vikki Ross
#thingsyouhearinagencies

ISBN: 978-1-326-14433-3

"Who wrote this?"

Nick Entwistle

Nick is the creative force behind the
Bank of Creativity and One Minute Briefs.
As well as producing concepts for major brands,
he delivers talks and workshops across the UK
and has had his work recognised by the likes of
Theo Paphitis, Pitch UK and Downing Street.

@BOC_ATM
@OneMinuteBriefs
interest@bankofcreativity.co.uk

Vikki Ross

Vikki brings copy to life for world-famous
brands and agencies. She wrote and judged the
D&AD New Blood 2014 Copywriting Brief and
judged the D&AD 2015 Writing for Advertising
category. She also tutors future creatives at
London's School of Communication Arts.

@VikkiRossWrites
vikkiross@hotmail.com

CONTENTS

FOREWORD

"I'm tweeting that"

It's funny the things you hear in agencies.
Ad speak, technical jargon, client feedback.
That's what we thought back in 2012 so we
created @AgencyQuotes on Twitter – a place
for everyone agency-side to celebrate the
advertising industry together and tweet all the
#thingsyouhearinagencies

Since then, we've shared almost 20,000 tweets
to over 7,000 followers around the world. We've
selected some of the best and put them in here
– our first book. You'll probably recognise a few.
You'll definitely nod knowingly. You may even
laugh. Just don't cry.

If you join in and share the
#thingsyouhearinagencies then thank you, this
book is for you. If you've never heard of the
hashtag and picked this book up by chance, then
thank you too. We truly appreciate everyone's
support and look forward to hearing more brilliant
agency quotes in the future.

@AgencyQuotes

"Run it by Legal"
No don't – it'll take ages to get signed off!
We've made every effort to include all Twitter names for the
tweets we've used, and we apologise for any unintentional mistakes.

7.

STUDIO

"I'm leaving early today, around 9pm."

- @rothbourne

"On a serious note, let's talk about the office slide."

- @bornengland

"Don't fire the staple gun, it's like a gun!"

- @JessieLRob

"Can you spray mount my turn-ups?"

- @Hazel_Pugh

"I've got a horrible feeling there's gonna be some late nights in this."

- @BOC_ATM

"The new girl's starting. Has anyone organised a ball for her to sit on?"

- @Guy_Vickerstaff

"Is my name all one word?"

- @PepperCorp

"Which meeting room is it - Draper or Stirling?"

- @AgencyQuotes

"Quick! Change the height on his chair, it'll be fucking hilarious."

- @MisterPritchard

"Don't go in the ladies' loo. There's a sheep in there."

- *@MrCCMiller*

TIMESHEETS

"How do I put 'hungover' in my timesheet?"

- @WorldOfOlly

"Those who don't fill their timesheets by Friday will not get Internet on Monday."

- *@theshwetamenon*

"Today we noticed you guys have never done your timesheets. Not a single one. Ever."

- *@FullFatEdam*

"Timesheets are literally the bane of my existence."

- @sarahjeansteele

"Please avoid using actual hours on your timesheet. You're making these accounts look unprofitable."

- @beaubodor

"I'll do my timesheet when I get the reminder email reminding me about the email reminding me to do my timesheet."

- @KatyWellhousen

"Hey, we're really gonna need you to enter your time job codes, they were due a month ago."

- *@jasondominy*

"I can't make lunch today, I've got timesheets coming out of my actual ass."

- *@supermantri*

"Explain how you logged 64 hours to design a logo."

- *@TalanaVB*

"If you don't fill in the last three months timesheets by tomorrow, your email will be blocked."

- *@nnulk*

"Does anybody know what I did on Tuesday?"

- *@BCLupton*

"What's the job number for doing your timesheets on your timesheets?"

- @BOC_ATM

ACCOUNTS

"Here's one the previous agency did that they really like."

- *@thebigcreative*

"Do you think the word 'free' is highlighted enough?"

- *@SarongJohnnie*

"Ideally we would emphasise our point of difference but we don't have one."

- @Dr_Draper

"Do you want me to do a brief? Or have you got enough to go on already?"

- *@rentaquill*

"Just get the project invoiced and started, we can work out what they need at the next meeting."

- *@stevewrigley*

"This proposition isn't single minded enough."

- *@StuandRob*

"Can you get my PA to book me a car? I need to attend that meeting about maximising agency profits."

- *@robsteeles*

"There isn't really a brief."

- @MyHouseofWords

"Lunch will be the quiet time you're looking for to really get this nailed."

- @MisterPritchard

"Does he look ABC1 enough?"

- @LiamLoanLack

"Don't forget we need to factor in a blame-storming session."

- @maccarants

"The target audience is everyone."

- @meganlucy1989

"Is it the one labelled final or final final or final v2.1_DON'T_SEND?"

- *@hannah_goes*

"This is nothing like Mad Men."

- *@calvin_barnett*

PLANNING

"Well, if you checked your work email over the weekend, we wouldn't be having this chat now."

- *@robsteeles*

"Are you a planner or a strategist? We need at least one of them."

- *@sankywashere*

38.

"Excel spreadsheets like a boss."

- @SayraMoran

"I can do any time except 3.30-4.30."
"Great, let's put it in for 3.30-4.30."

- @ABlakeley

"Don't spend any time on it."

- @dognbonesjones

"I didn't get your email."
"You replied to it."

- @MrCCMiller

"It's a tiny tiny job. It will take you literally just a second to do."

- @ilungaize

"He has the whole Planner effectiveness thing going on. Look at that quadrant of effectiveness."

- @markhadfield

"We are where we are."

- @Whatleydude

"We've got a load of amends, there's been a planner in the works."

- @nicktuckwood

JARGON

"Customers are undertaking platform-agnostic journeys."

- *@stuartknapman*

"All millennials can create GIFS!"

- *@bbdperfectstorm*

"I need a more comfortable chair... I reckon it'll help me ideate."

- *@AgencyQuotes*

"Multiglobality."

- *@LucianTrestler*

"We'd like to introduce you to our new Head of Emerging and Integrated Development and Creative Strategy."

- *@TheRealSheaB*

48.

"Could you be hyperspecific?"

- *@Mededitor*

"What on earth is blue sky thinking and why is that vanilla?"

- *@strattoncraig*

"Let's push the envelope and think outside the box."

- @STEcopywriting

"I need a millennial!"

- @Jacquelafay

50.

"That's right up there with webinar in the marketing speak shit list."

- *@GDAcreative*

GUIDELINES

"They're guidelines, not 'in-stone' lines."

- *@copywriterLDN*

"Looks like the objective of these brand guidelines was to get the word 'consistent' on every page."

- *@AgencyQuotes*

"Oh, they're just the brand guidelines. We don't bother with them."

- @bravenewmalden

"Do we have a best practices guide for the best practices guide?"

- @cwilmc

"It's fine for it to be off brand."

- @AgencyQuotes

"It's taken them five months to write a style guide."

- @AgencyQuotes

"We don't believe in using brand guidelines... we want to be different."

- @AdUtopia72

"Whoever is printing out the 180 page brand guidelines doc, you deserve a painful death."

- @tompeters22

**"Brand guidelines?
That's still a thing?"**

- *@noopurvasuraj*

**"The brand personality is
cheeky but formal."**

- *@AgencyQuotes*

COPY

"This SMS copy needs to sound more premium."

- *@SpecialK_2311*

"Can we knock half the words out?"

- *@OneMinuteBriefs*

"The client likes the headline, but could you add these five points into it?"

- @Matty_J_B

"The client wants it written exactly how they've sent it over, but shorter."

- *@WorldOfOlly*

"Just make it up."

- *@re_scrawl*

"They don't mind a dirty headline."

- @bravenewmalden

"Can you remove the Lorem Ipsum text from the designs, this is not approved copy."

- @HannahLouisa_xo

"They love the copy, but think it might be a bit clever for the target audience."

- *@owenjevans*

"Just fill it with some English."

- *@theshwetamenon*

"Please don't make me write in Excel."

- @VikkiRossWrites

"The client has written some copy. I don't think we can push back on it."

- @undercoverman

"Lets caveat the shit out of it."

- *@ludoyouknow*

"The client loves your lines, and they've suggested a few of their own."

- *@tomcopy*

"Flesh out the copy but keep to the same word length."

- *@bravenewmalden*

"Is that headline too clever, or not clever enough?"

- *@awlilnatty*

"Can we put the language of concept A with the design of concept B?"

- *@tweetXXVI*

70.

**"Nobody reads
the copy anyway."**

- @portishair

**"The client's asked if we
could write the copy in
English instead of Latin."**

- @andsomepeople

DESIGN

"Can you photoshop the car, turn it round so it's facing the front more?"

- @mandyfleetwood

"We'll worry about that in production."

- @DDBChicago

74.

"I think this red needs to be more blue."

- *@jonathanend*

"I'm not too happy with the Pantone ref of this brew."

- *@LarnerC*

"I need you to work in this tin foil covered closet for the next week."

- @StanRizzo_SCDP

"What do you mean it's not broadcast quality? It looks fine on my laptop."

- @EdScottLondon

"Can we take out the apostrophe? It looks ugly."

- @Dr_Draper

"Can you make the black darker?"

- @copybeard

"Work your magic."

- @reubenturner

"Make the shadows white."

- *@LukeBonner*

"It needs to look organic, but clumsy."

- *@adlandjones*

"And then we just need some experiential wank."

- @JamesDawe3

"Could the text box be jazzed up a little?"

- @dognbonesjones

80.

"I don't get paid enough to use PowerPoint."

- *@awlilnatty*

"Make it pop."

- *@Mededitor*

"You know, I kind of liked the way it looked before."

- @NickCanDo

"Do we have a final FINAL v2 latest final USE THIS ONE version of the logo?"

- @CookiesForDevo

"Can you
write some
bollocks for me
to explain why
this looks
the way it does?"

- @bornengland

FONT

"It's a typocalypse!"

- *@bobblebardsley*

"Kern kern kern!"

- *@RaviGopar*

"You change that font and I'll change your face."

- *@Wavey_Gravy*

"Just craft the kerning between the r and n. It looks like bum."

- *@BOC_ATM*

"They don't like the font."
"It's their font."

- @MrAndyPowell

"Just use Helvetica, you can't go wrong."

- @BOC_ATM

"I prefer that you read it, rather than me presenting it. I can't present in Helvetica."

- @BruckAndFontes

"Times New Roman is the Devil's font."

- @Wooldebeast

"All I want is comic serif."

- @rosst63

90.

"What typeface do you think of when you think of cats?"

- @_ilovebadgers_

"Helvetica is The Beatles of typefaces."

- @lmcdesignltd

SOCIAL

"How can we make this tweet social?"

- *@Jason_scott*

"Yeah... but is it hashtaggable?"

- *@restreitinho*

"That's the problem with Instagram: you see stuff."

- *@ostreetstudio*

"Can we change the colour of the Facebook and Twitter logos?"

- *@bravenewmalden*

"Make the hashtag trend."

- @twietie88

**"I WhatsApp'd
the client."**

- *@gsenev*

**"Snatchchat, or whatever
the next big thing is."**

- *@aStoltze*

DATA

"So if data is king then surely big data must be fucking King Kong."

- @DGMediaGuru

"Your data is dated"

- @BOC_ATM

100.

"Can't you just geo-tag the spunk bubble?"

- @LeeRobinsDesign

"Big ideas need big code."

- @scottcouper

"Ah the power seat. Can you feel the data flowing through you?"

- @_eltee

"Don't be a data hater"

- @AgencyQuotes

"Data beats opinion any day. But opinion layered over data is epic."

- @picturpoet

DIGITAL

"This is killing my ram."

- @BigBrandIdeas

"For a digital agency, we get too many paper cuts."

- *@dennistejero*

"I'm glad you're not in this edit, it's like a digital slaughterhouse."

- *@LucyDelilahB*

"I like this layout of,
what is it called?
Yes, Wireframe.
But I think it's too grey."

- @DDBChicago

"Sometimes I click on ads
just to make them pay."

- @kirstycarrot

108.

**"Oh yes.
I forgot about Google."**

- *@twietie88*

**"…And then they'll all
come to the website and
engage with us there."**

- *@DDBChicago*

PITCH

"The client said we were a very close second in the pitch."

- @AgencyQuotes

"I got 99 problems but a pitch ain't one."

- @ShittyFuture

"It's his pitch-winning dance."

- @PWCFreelance

"We lost the pitch
because they
shat themselves
and didn't take
the best idea."

- @BOC_ATM

"You have to pay to get
into the pitch and the
client owns any ideas
generated, even if we
don't get chosen?"

- @designByRamox

SHOOTS

"I shot her last night."

- @BOC_ATM

"The pancakes are for a shoot, can you please stop eating them."

- @ABlakeley

116.

"I want sexy, think of me in Speedos and you're there."

- *@rpmltd*

"We are going to shoot the shit out of it."

- *@mattlynch_honda*

"Has anyone seen a Light Saber lying around?"

- *@GreyLondon*

FEEDBACK

"We haven't had any feedback from the client yet but then again... we haven't sent them any work."

- @joemakingsense

"Here we go - art direction by numbers."

- @AgencyQuotes

120.

"We're waiting on feedback on the feedback's feedback."

- *@wheelswordsmith*

"After a lot of deliberation, we think we should go back to the previous edit."

- @HashmukhKerai

"The client wants the opening para to be more on brand."
"It's taken from their homepage."

- @MrAndyPowell

"The feedback doc is so big, they're sending it on WeTransfer."

- *@AgencyQuotes*

"How am I supposed to come up with award-winning ideas if we keep getting client feedback?"

- *@dimasnovriandi*

"They want something disruptive. Ish."

- *@AgencyQuotes*

"Why the fuck do they send feedback in Excel? No normal person fucking uses fucking Excel."

- *@AgencyQuotes*

CLIENTS

"Hide all that.
The client's coming
in this morning."

- @AgencyQuotes

"The client emptied all of our hotel minibars. They know what we're like."

- @aboudcreative

"The client doesn't like the word 'kickstart'."

- @jialehh

"That line
the client really
liked yesterday?
They don't like
it any more."

- *@welchwords*

"The client is asking if we can just use free images."

- @_TerrySmith_

"What are the specs for the ad you've booked?" "You decide."

- @Carlie5

**"We'll need to Mac concepts up...
the client doesn't understand scamps."**

- *@RobertoHaino*

**"They haven't
got the budget."**

- *@WSS_Design*

"The client made me do it."

- @KatyWellhousen

MEETINGS

"How'd your breakfast meeting go?"
"Good!
We each had seven shots of tequila."

- @marionlow1

"I don't want to have a meeting for the sake of a meeting but let's put something in the diary."

- *@hannah_goes*

"We're brainstorming but not."

- *@AgencyQuotes*

"Do I need to be in this meeting?"

- *@ABlakeley*

"It's a thought shower, not a brainstorm."

- *@DBDsearch*

"I think we
need to meet
to decide when
to meet."

- @DDBChicago

PRESENTATIONS

"I judge people from their first three slides."

- @jonathanend

"Death by PowerPoint
is happening in the
boardroom in
10 minutes."

- @AgencyQuotes

"It's about different
things interacting with
different things in
different ways."

- @thatbrandguy

"Are you working on the mega deck?"

- *@helloThatSaid*

"We spent last night editing the presentation and we've got it down to 120 slides."

- *@thatbrandguy*

144.

"Where's my presenting shirt?"

- @AgencyQuotes

FRIDAY

"Yeah I'll do it... on Monday."

- @songforlo

"Lunch with him was kinda like being water boarded with pinot noir."

- *@adisruptivetype*

"Pint?"

- *@CatherineAnnR*

**"I won't drink tonight...
I'll probably just have a
bottle of wine."**

- @CharlieRiggall

**"Care for a drink?
Let me top off your glass.
We need more vodka.
Oh wait, that's just
Sterling's office."**

- @PeteCampbell_NY

150.

"After last night there's no chance I'm going out tonight. Ok, I'll stay for one."

- *@WorldOfOlly*

"The beer trolley is late."

- *@nicktuckwood*

"Let's go drink beer and eat lobster."

- @RossMacDonaldW6

"Going for lunch with a client on a Friday means see you on Monday."

- @ColTalbot1

"Obviously you don't have to work on the weekend, but we need it by 9am Monday."

- *@hannah_goes*

DEADLINES

"There's no deadline so just keep going til you get another brief."

- @AgencyQuotes

"When's the deadline?"
"Last Thursday."

- @OneMinuteBriefs

156.

"No, you can't miss that false deadline. "

- *@JamesDawe3*

"So when's the real deadline?"

- *@mattpooley*

"It needs to be done as of yesterday."

- *@sidhshuk*

CHRISTMAS

"Client says can we put a Santa hat on the logo?"

- @arminthedoor

"That's my last deck of the year, people."

- *@markhadfield*

"They want us to say 'Christmas' in the headline."

- *@AgencyQuotes*

"All I want for Christmas is to never have to fill out a timesheet again ever."

- *@KatyWellhousen*

"Who wants to see the video from the Christmas party?"

- *@AgencyQuotes*

162.

"That red doesn't look very festive."

- @AgencyQuotes

"I don't like this Jesus/Santa thing. We need a single brand advocate."

- @tomcopy

"Make it look colder."

- @AgencyQuotes

"No no no!
Who wants to open a
PowerPoint document
on Christmas Eve?"

- *@PaulStayt*

"I'm moving Christmas
to Monday."

- *@Meadows148*

"It is always Christmas."

- @LaurenDig

"They didn't give us a parsnip Pantone."

- @zeroabovealex

"What font would Father Christmas use?"

- @JordonMann

"Will there be another version?"

Yes, it doesn't stop here...
Head to @AgencyQuotes to
tell us more #thingsyouhearinagencies
and you might just feature in our next book.
Thanks for reading.

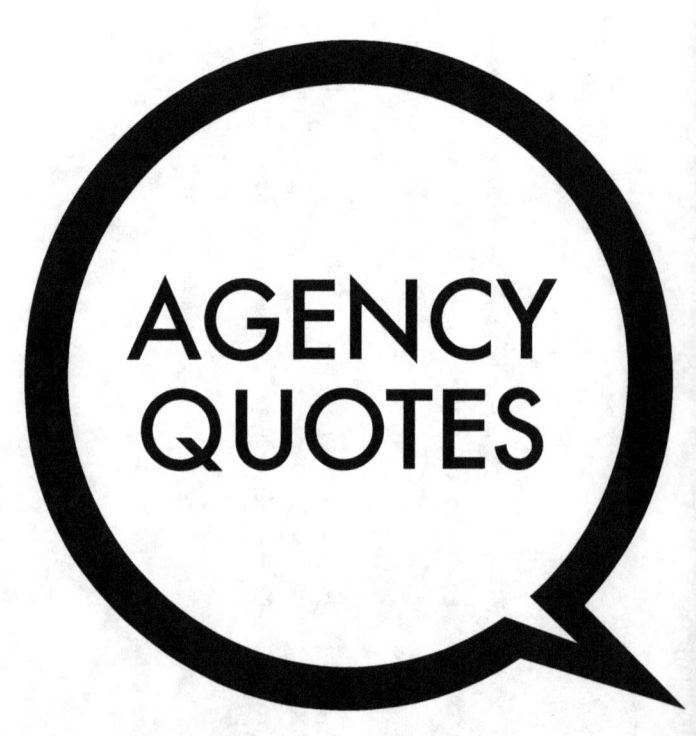

AGENCY QUOTES

www.ingramcontent.com/pod-product-compliance
Lightning Source LLC
Chambersburg PA
CBHW060850170526
45158CB00001B/296